TO: Joe, Tabitha + Marsily

FROM: Marge Potts

(5-12-09)

WHEN I GET WHERE I'M GOING

RIVERS RUTHERFORD & GEORGE TEREN

RUTLEDGE HILL PRESS | NASHVILLE, TENNESSEE

A DIVISION OF THOMAS NELSON PUBLISHERS | WWW.THOMASNELSON.COM

FROM RIVERS: FOR MY GRANDFATHER, A MAN WHO LOVED JESUS AND WHO LOVED ME,
AND WHO IS NO DOUBT IN HEAVEN RIGHT NOW TELLING EVERYONE
HOW THINGS SHOULD BE RUN.

FROM GEORGE: FOR MY FAMILY, THOSE HERE WHO KEEP ME GOING AND
THOSE WHO HAVE ALREADY GOTTEN THERE.

PHOTO OF BRAD PAISLEY ON PAGE V BY JIM SHEA, COPYRIGHT © 2006

PUBLISHED BY RUTLEDGE HILL PRESS, A DIVISION OF THOMAS NELSON, INC., P.O. BOX 141000, NASHVILLE, TENNESSEE 37214.

ART DIRECTION AND DESIGN BY DON BAILEY FOR BAILEY DESIGN, NASHVILLE, TN.

RUTLEDGE HILL PRESS BOOKS MAY BE PURCHASED IN BULK FOR EDUCATIONAL, BUSINESS, FUND-RAISING,
OR SALES PROMOTIONAL USE. FOR INFORMATION, PLEASE E-MAIL SPECIALMARKETS@THOMASNELSON.COM.

ISBN 10 — 1-4016-0323-8
ISBN 13 — 978-1-4016-0323-6

PRINTED IN THE UNITED STATES OF AMERICA
07 08 09 10—5 4 3 2

THE FIRST TIME I HEARD
"WHEN I GET WHERE I'M GOING,"

I remember having the same reaction that countless fans have described to me. I thought about someone I had lost in my life, about the things they must be doing now that their soul is free, and I felt tremendous hope. The song brings on a sense of closure for me, of understanding in the midst of the unfathomable. It sums up the full-circle journey of life like countless songs have done throughout music history, but in a more poetic and beautiful way. Rivers and George have written a masterpiece. This book is a celebration of a piece of art that has consoled people in their grief, graced several memorial services, and brought back fond memories. I personally don't think there has ever been a finer song about this subject. I am honored to have been the person you first heard singing these words.

BRAD PAISLEY

THERE IS SO MUCH TO SAY.

And yet it is hard to know what to say.
Words seem so inadequate and too one-dimensional
to express sorrow for your loss.

While words may not be enough, it is our hope that the images and
sentiments in the pages of this book and in the song that inspired it can
bring you some comfort in the weeks and months ahead.

LIFE IS PRECIOUS.

LOVE IS ETERNAL.

DEATH IS
MERELY A DOOR
SEPARATING
WHERE WE ARE
FROM
WHERE WE ARE GOING.

DON'T BELIEVE FOR ONE MINUTE THAT THIS IS IT—THAT WE DIE AND IT'S OVER. THAT WE ARE BRIEF INHABITANTS OF A PLANET THAT IS NOTHING MORE THAN A SPECK OF DUST AFLOAT IN A VAST, COLD, EMPTY VOID.

THERE IS SO MUCH MORE.
WE WILL GO ON FOREVER.

THE UNIVERSE WAS NOT SET UP TO ACCOMMODATE THE IDEA THAT
SOMETHING CAN COME FROM NOTHING,
NOR THAT SOMETHING CAN COME TO NOTHING.

THE PART OF US THAT PUTS THE SPARKLE IN THE EYE OF A DELIGHTED CHILD, THE LIGHT THAT IS UNIQUE IN EVERY PERSON, THE THING THAT MAKES EACH INDIVIDUAL SPECIAL—

IT GOES ON.

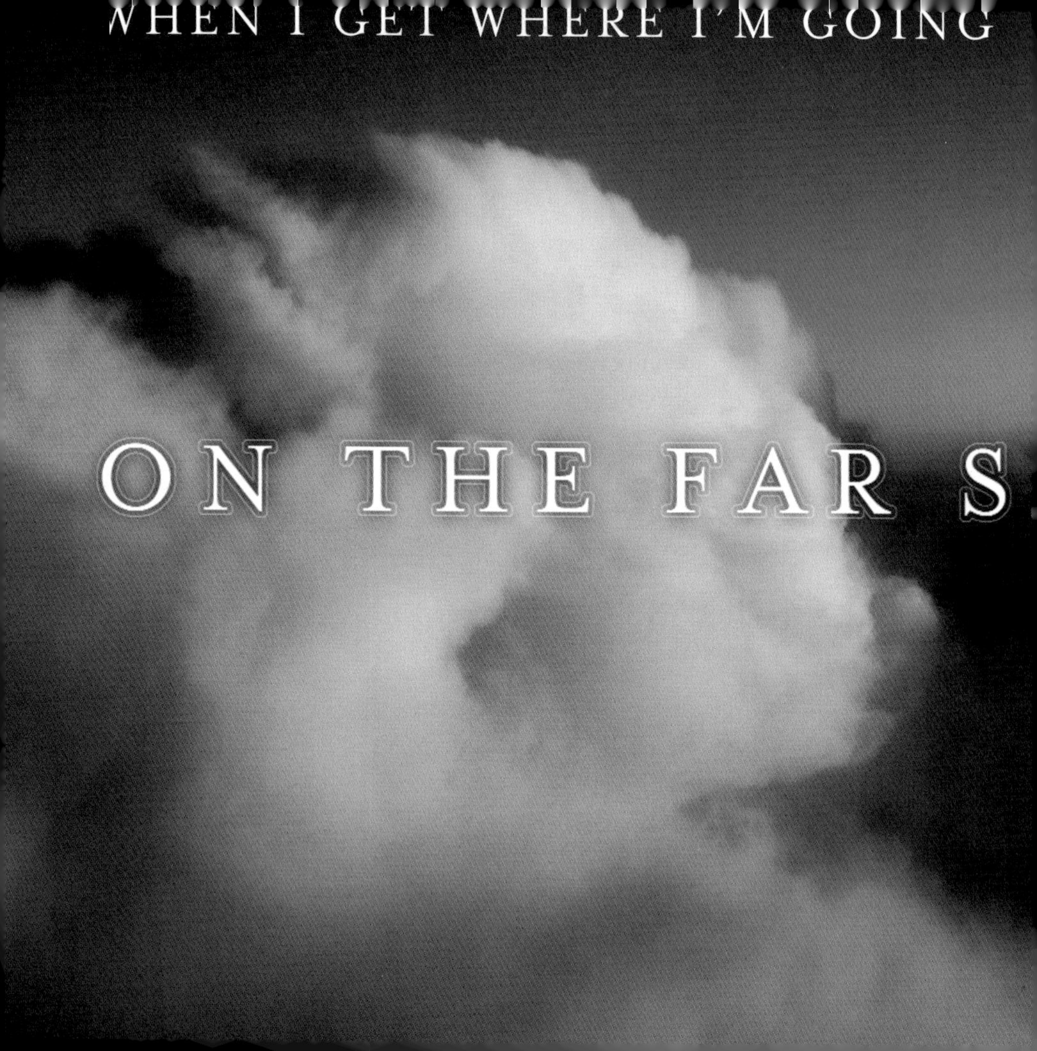
WHEN I GET WHERE I'M GOING
ON THE FAR S

IT'S ALL PART OF THE JOURNEY . . .

FROM THE FIRST BREATH, FIRST SMILE, FIRST STEP,
TO THE FIRST DAY OF SCHOOL.
FIRST FRIEND. FIRST NIGHT AWAY FROM HOME.

ALL PART OF THE JOURNEY.

THE DISAPPOINTMENT OF BEING CUT FROM THE TEAM AFTER
MONTHS OF PRACTICE. THE EUPHORIA OF A FIRST-EVER KISS AND
THE REALIZATION THAT THERE IS A LOT MORE TO THE OPPOSITE
SEX THAN WAS EVER SUSPECTED. THE BITTERSWEET SEPARATION
FROM LONGTIME FRIENDS UPON GRADUATION.

ALL A PART OF THE JOURNEY.

THE CHANCES NOT TAKEN.
THE LOVES THAT WEREN'T PURSUED.
THE DOUBTS, THE MISTAKES,
THE WOULD'VES, COULD'VES, AND SHOULD'VES.
SHAME, REGRET, DOUBT, GUILT, SELFISHNESS.

PAINFUL, BUT PART OF IT.

THE GOOD FEELING THAT COMES
FROM GIVING A BOX FULL OF TOYS
TO THE CHRISTMAS DRIVE AT CHURCH.
THE PRIDE OF BEING HIRED FOR YOUR
FIRST JOB. THE FIRST RAISE.
THE OLD VW YOU BOUGHT WITH
YOUR OWN MONEY.
THE TWO WEEKS YOU SPENT TOURING EUROPE.

DEVELOPING A MORAL COMPASS.
FINDING FAITH, BUILDING UPON IT,
AND DRAWING FROM IT.

ALL PART OF THE JOURNEY.

BAPTISM. GRADUATION. MARRIAGE.
PARENTHOOD.
DIVORCE. EARLY RETIREMENT. EXPLORING, CHALLENGING, REACHING, CRASHING. BABY STEPS, GIANT STEPS, AND MISSTEPS. PUTTING YOUR FOOT IN YOUR MOUTH. ALL THE RANDOM, CRAZY, SEEMINGLY UNRELATED, SOMETIMES UNFAIR, SOMETIMES SERENDIPITOUS, MARVELOUS, MADDENING,

AMAZING EVENTS THAT MAKE UP A LIFE.

LAUGHING, HURTING, WANTING, GIVING, DREAMING, LOVING, CRYING, AND . . .

DYING.
PART OF THE JOURNEY.
THE ONE STEP WE ALL MAKE.

THE FINAL STEP. WHEN ALL THE RANDOMNESS
AND CRAZINESS, ALL THE PAINFUL LESSONS,
THE SINS AND STRUGGLES,
THE VICTORIES AND SUCCESSES OF OUR JOURNEY
FINALLY MAKE SENSE AND TAKE ON PERSPECTIVE.

IT'S ALL PART OF THE JOURNEY,
A JOURNEY OF JOY AND SUFFERING.

BUT SUFFERING PRODUCES PERSEVERANCE,
WHICH PRODUCES CHARACTER,

WHICH PRODUCES HOPE.

I HOPE

that in this difficult time you find comfort
in the presence of your Creator.
I hope you know that you are loved.

I HOPE

that in the midst of your loss
you can enjoy and
celebrate the memories.

I HOPE

that, in the end,
you will find your faith to be
strong and sustaining.

I HOPE

that in the quietest corner of your soul,
you can rest in the knowledge
that you and the person you lost
will be together again.

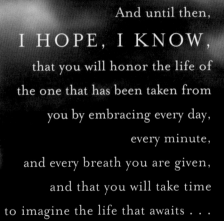

And until then,

I HOPE, I KNOW,

that you will honor the life of

the one that has been taken from

you by embracing every day,

every minute,

and every breath you are given,

and that you will take time

to imagine the life that awaits . . .

I'M GONNA LAND

RUN MY FINGERS

. . . AND RIDE A

BESIDE A LION

THROUGH HIS MANE

DROP OF RAIN

IMAGINE

THAT DYING IS

ONLY THE BEGINNING.

THAT LIFE ON EARTH IS ONLY A PRELUDE TO
A SPECTACULAR SYMPHONY.

ENDLESS POSSIBILITIES

A place where you can spread your wings ,

Ride a raindrop,

Run your fingers through a lion's mane.

A place where all worldly limitations and

I M A

shortcomings have been left behind.

All sins forgiven.

All questions answered.

A state of permanent grace.

NO HATE. NO PAIN.
NO CONFLICT. NO REGRET.

IMAGINE

COMPLETE AND TOTAL FREEDOM,

UNBOUNDED HOPE,

THE IMPOSSIBLE BEING POSSIBLE.

MEETING YOUR MAKER FACE TO FACE

AND REALIZING

THAT YOU HAVE BEEN MADE LIKE HIM.

AN ASCENDANCE IN EVERY SENSE OF THE WORD

TO A HIGHER PLACE, CLOSER TO GOD.

SIMPLER, PURER, VOID OF PRETENSE,

AND PRESUMPTION.

CLOSE YOUR EYES AND REMEMBER YOUR SWEETEST SUCCESS

Your most loving moment

The greatest kindness ever paid to you

HEAVEN IS EMINENTLY SWEETER, GREATER, AND MORE LOVING

IN HEAVEN, WE ARE FREE TO . . .

GIVE WITHOUT FEAR OF NOT HAVING ENOUGH
LOVE WITHOUT FEAR OF REJECTION
REACH WITHOUT FEAR OF FALLING
EXPLORE WITHOUT FEAR OF LOSING OUR WAY
STAND WITHOUT FEAR OF RIDICULE
FORGIVE WITHOUT FEAR OF BEING HURT AGAIN
CONFESS WITHOUT FEAR OF REPRISAL
SUBMIT WITHOUT FEAR OF APPEARING WEAK

NOT TO MENTION . . .

BELIEVE, LAUGH, SING, DANCE, ENJOY, LOAF, CLIMB, SOMERSAULT, SAIL, WRITE, ASK, ENCOURAGE, WALK, RUN, LISTEN, WATCH, LOAN, PLAY, WORK, WHISTLE, JUGGLE, RECREATE, CELEBRATE, ORIGINATE, IMITATE, OVERLOOK, UNDERSTAND, WORK AROUND, FOLLOW THROUGH,

AND DO. AND BE. IN PEACE.

FREE.

IMAGINE.

SO MUCH PAIN AND SO

IN THIS WORLD W

MUCH DARKNESS

TUMBLE THROUGH...

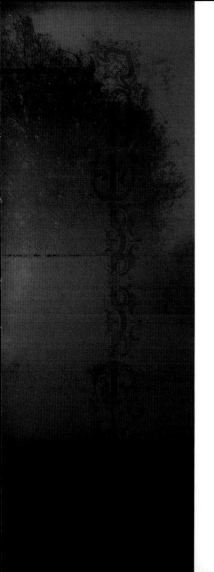

FAITH IS THE LIGHT OF THE SOUL IN A DARK AND TROUBLED WORLD.

FAITH IS WHAT GUARDS OUR CONVICTIONS.
IT IS THE ASSURANCE OF THINGS
WE CANNOT SEE AND THAT
WHICH WE HAVEN'T EXPERIENCED.
IT IS NOT A BLIND LEAP INTO A DARK HOLE.
FAITH IS A REASONABLE BELIEF IN TRUTH,
BEAUTY, JUSTICE, AND GRACE.

FAITH EXPECTS THE IMMEASURABLE,

THE UNPROVABLE, THE INVISIBLE, THE BETTER.

FAITH IS WHAT ALLOWS US TO LOVE, AND IT IS WHAT HELPS US LET GO.

FAITH MAKES IT POSSIBLE
TO ACCEPT THAT WHICH WE CAN'T
UNDERSTAND.

ALL THESE QUESTIONS

AND SO MUCH

NS I CAN'T ANSWER

WORK TO DO

DRIVEN BY DREAMS

FUELED BY HOPE

SPARKED BY CURIOSITY

TESTED BY ADVERSITY

SHAPED BY EXPERIENCE

SUSTAINED BY FAITH

WE LIVE.

THE SKILLS WE LEARN

THE COLORS WE SEE

THE FLAVORS WE TASTE

THE FRIENDS WE MAKE

THE LIVES WE TOUCH

THE SUCCESSES WE HAVE

WE GROW.

OUR MINDS EXPAND

OUR HORIZONS BROADEN

OUR ROOTS DEEPEN

OUR RELATIONSHIPS STRENGTHEN

OUR UNDERSTANDING INCREASES

OUR LIVES BECOME MORE MEANINGFUL

OUR

JOURNEY

IS

OUR

LIFE

THERE IS JOY
THERE IS HEARTBREAK
THERE ARE SETBACKS
THERE ARE DIFFICULT CHOICES
THERE IS REGRET
BUT THERE IS A DESTINATION

AN END TO OUR JOURNEY ON EARTH

THE BEGINNING OF
OUR JOURNEY
IN ETERNITY

DON'T BELIEVE FOR ONE MINUTE THAT THIS IS IT.

HOLD ON TO HOPE. LEAN ON FAITH. IMAGINE.

I WILL SEE M

AND I'LL STAND FO

OF HIS AMA

MAKER'S FACE

VER IN THE LIGHT

ING GRACE

"I AM FREE!"

"I'VE BEEN SPRUNG FROM THE LIMITS OF TIME AND SPACE AND I AM
WHAT I WAS ORIGINALLY INTENDED TO BE."

"I AM HERE AND YOU CAN'T
IMAGINE HOW INCREDIBLE IT IS."

"BECAUSE I NO LONGER SUFFER,
I AM NOT AFRAID OF ANYTHING."

"I CAN TRY EVERYTHING I'VE EVER WANTED TO TRY.
HAVE YOU EVER SEEN THE INSIDE OF A VOLCANO?
DANCED ON NEPTUNE?
WATCHED A BABY BUMBLEBEE BEING BORN?
I HAVE."

"MY ARMS, MY LEGS, MY EYES, MY BRAIN, MY EARS,
EVERYTHING IS AS IT WAS ORIGINALLY DESIGNED.
NO DEFECTS. NO WEAR. NO TEAR. NO LIMITS."

"WHEN I RUN, I DON'T GET TIRED.
WHEN I FALL, IT DOESN'T HURT."

"I HAVE MET MY MAKER AND HE IS
BIGGER, GRANDER, MORE BEAUTIFUL, MORE COMPASSIONATE,
MORE JUST THAN I COULD BEGIN TO DESCRIBE.
HE IS GOOD.

I ASSURE YOU I AM SAFE
AND CONTENT IN HIS PRESENCE."

"AND . . .
HE LOVES YOU AND WANTS TO HELP YOU COPE WITH LOSING ME."

"AS YOU GO THROUGH YOUR LIFE,
THERE WILL BE THINGS YOU WISH YOU COULD SHARE WITH ME.

LITTLE TRIUMPHS.
FIRSTS.
FUNNY STORIES.

WELL, YOU MAY NOT KNOW IT,
BUT I'LL KNOW.

AND IF YOU FEEL THE NEED TO TELL ME ANYWAY,
THAT'S GOOD TOO."

"I KNOW YOU ARE GOING TO MISS ME,
AND I'M GLAD.
BE ANGRY.
CRY.
BUT DON'T DO IT FOR ME.
DO IT FOR YOU, BECAUSE I AM HAPPIER AND MORE FULFILLED
THAN I EVER WAS ON EARTH."

"I AM AT PEACE."